FROM HEART 2 SOUL 2 HEAVEN

EDITED BY JONATHAN MBOYO

From Heart 2 Soul 2 Heaven Copyright © 2015 by Jonathan Mboyo

All rights reserved. This book or any portion thereof may not be reproduced or used in any manner whatsoever without the express written permission of the publisher except for the use of brief quotations in a book review or scholarly journal.

First Printing: 2015

ISBN 978-1-326-10946-2

Contents

Acknowledgments…………………………..4

Introduction………………………………...5

Chapter 1: Prayers…………………..……6

Chapter 2: Poetic Proverbs of My Faith…..15

Acknowledgments

I want to thank New Harvest Christian Fellowship community and all the Christians I have ever met who served as a good example and part of the inspiration that they gave me for this book through Testimonies & Fellowship, as for names I should at least mention a few. My mother for her prayers for me to get saved thank God she did.

Peter my best friend has given me great support, firecracker Manny a true servant of God, Dany a man truly on fire for God and Pastor Tim and The Madera & Fresno New Harvest Christian Fellowship in America they have been truly a blessing from God. To those who I have not mentioned by name tough luck! Just joking your names may not be a part of the book but part of your faith & wisdom in the things of God is so chin up. I want to especially thank Iván Guaderrama for allowing me to use his painting "with a vibrant heart" for this book cover and is inspirational Christian art I urge people to be inspired by taking a look at more of his art (http://www.ivanguaderrama.com/)

And saving the best for last I thank God for the great inspiration the reason I wrote this book for and stepped out of my comfort zone to do so I praise and worship him and let his glory be known thru this book and Jesus inspire & save souls for there is no fault in you and the life you led ho kurios mou kai ho theos mou

Introduction

I write this book in a form of prayers, words spoken in faith of my concerns, joy I have found in him, my hopes, praise to him, fears and my faith in him through the good news taught by Jesus Christ my Lord and Saviour. I do this rather than just pray and keep it at that because this focuses my mind more on him and that's how this whole book got started. And so as you can imagine it will get quite personal, and the subject ranges into many avenues of my faith.

I hope it helps and inspire someone's Faith, Oh by the way I know the rhetoric sounds kind of cheesy or Outdated but….Its more meaningful to pray and write this way for me because its poetic in sense, which conveys seriousness and emotion in a deeper way which I could say is the way I like to communicate with God.

Chapter 1: Prayers

Prayer of worship

I humble myself before you Lord and ask for your presence to worship you because I am thankful for your hand of grace & sovereignty placed on my life, my health for one, in the 24 years I have walked this earth rare as it been that I have had any medical treatment, or even step foot in a hospital for my own needs or others close to me. If that is not a blessing I don't know what is. Glory to God As I sleep and walk in the world always he protected me sheltered me from harm, Therefore I do not make complaints because I'm blessed even though I do not deserve it, Glory to God for such grace. When I do it comes to focus the error of my ways, when I see the injustice and cruelty of the world I think that could easily be me.

In the name of Jesus thankful I am for all the meals I have ever had even when money was tight never in my life have I never gone to bed hungry because of food shortage, if that is not a blessing what is? Alas I find myself smirking and joyful because the Simple truth **I AM BLESSED!** And in the name of Jesus I pray Amen!

Talking 2 God: The Grand weaver[1]

You are my point of reference when one asks "who loves without hating? Who loves those who hate him?" I pray see about them in their heart of hearts. You come to mind when one asks "who in this world is just and discerns between what is truly right and wrong and with sovereignty abides by it? Is there really one out there who cannot be tainted by corruption? I pray reveal yourself to those who seek you like I once did and bring meaning & fulfilment to their mind & souls as you lead them through the destiny of their lives Amen.

---

1. Dr. Ravi Zacharias RZIM

Prayer of Concern & Faith

Father God I pray for protection from the strategies of the enemy of my soul, for he attacks my mind with thoughts to try and turn me against you Father, thoughts that attempt to question my faith and whether or not I can live to the image set by your son. But he fails because you know me when I give tithe I give faithfully, when kneel before you at the altar I do so faithfully, when I discuss of your word with fellow believers I do so with faith and when I do work that is needed at your house of worship I do so joyfully and faithfully. And so if his strategy is to cast doubt it won't work for I believe in you Lord and your word and if I did not there would be no joy when I serve at your house of worship, or any meaning in the obedience of your word without faith just an act of futility and a waste of your time. But as you know my heart & soul you know it is not so, therefor I rebuke the enemy and his lies and continue in my pursuit of you and I pray your spirit strengthens my faith. For I serve you as a loving son of the living God, I as a man have hard time expressing my feelings sometimes but I know through Christ all things are possible so these concerns of mine I put to you and I know you will lift these burdens if I put it up to your son. He will lift these heavy burdens of my shoulders like they are luggage and I will sign them off to him in a covenant with my signature "Jonathan Mboyo in God I trust" and then they'll be taken away just like that, for I know you are always faithful to your people and so just by saying this prayer it puts my mind at ease and I patiently wait **"Philippians 2:6-11: Who being in the form of God, did not consider it robbery to be equal with God but made Himself of no reputation, taking the form of a bondservant, and coming in the likeness of men. And being found in appearance as a man, He humbled Himself and became obedient to the point of death, even the death of the cross. Therefore God also has highly exalted Him and given Him the name which is above every name, that at the name of Jesus every knee should bow, of those in heaven, and of those on earth, and of those under the earth, and every tongue should confess that Jesus Christ is Lord, to the glory of God the Farther".** In God I trust and in the name of Jesus I pray Amen!

Prayer of Joy

In the name of Jesus who my aim is to be, I pray, when it comes to joy I have found in him many things suddenly come to mind. I could express it through song but my voice sounds like a bag of cats being swung violently, no dancing for me either I think but I serve a living God who as gave me joy so I know you'll help in those very unfortunate areas of mine while I still continue to praise and worship. You have allowed me to express my joy through fellowship with fellow believers in doing so I have been encouraged by their words and support and hopefully I have done so the same for them, to know I am not alone in this journey is a relief. To speak to people from different walks of life come together in faith lifts my spirits because isolation and no house of worship to be alone in this world can only bring corruption which breeds sin and then for that soul to be cast below and I believe this is so earnestly. So for me to have such great fellowship **I SAY PRAISE THE LORD!** And in doing so, I hope that even the angels in heaven join me in praise and rejoice of the father. One joyous moment I never praised you for, being a child you amazed me with the creation of this world and opened my eyes to it, the sight of a beauteous sun set as I remember a humongous blazing orange visage as it mixed with the fading blue sky as I stood in awe I had no words just mesmerised and in trance as it slowly began to set as if it was disappearing into the earth. The darkness creeped in and the sky was no longer blue but darkened with a faint orange. The sun was the only light in the sky; street lights light a path forward to it. I felt so close to it. Yet it made me feel so small, I felt as though if I reached out my hand I could touch it. I felt as though if I walked towards it I could reach it, even though thinking in such ways made no sense. Back then amazing or something or other might have come to mind but now all I have to say is **IN THE BEGINNING GOD!**

Prayer for Family, Friends & My church

Lord I pray for my family I pray that you protect them minister to them and bring them closer to you Lord. Anoint them with the Holy Spirit keep them in mind and save their souls & show them the love, mercy, patience and grace you have shown me that the house we break bread in and sleep in be blessed by you father. I pray Jesus for my friends who are not yet saved I pray that one day your will be done and reach them and their families I hate the thought of them not having their living souls saved I pray for my ally who supported my decision to give my life to Jesus who's encouragement helped me be true to myself and in that truth I found you God. I Pray that you bless him work through him, give him patience & knowledge and understanding and bring him closer to you remove the heavy bindings that hold him in worldly things and instead allow him to use those bindings in your name to bind the evil of this world and then let it be that those bindings be anchor that weighs down the adversary and then cast him and his sins to the furnace. Never have I been a man of many words and you know this but I require your guidance so I speak to you through payer and again I pray for my friend this time for his family that you may use him to reach his family and bring them together in your name under your house for your Glory. In your house of worship I pray for more friends at the church to strengthen our faith for you to meet their needs you know their hearts so I know it will be done healing, blessings, gifts given through Holy Spirit to those who pray for them and bring peace of mind to your faithful servants. In your name Lord and the name of your son Jesus I pray for my church I pray simply that your will be done that more souls are saved more needs are met that you anoint us with your will thru the Holy Spirit. As soon as I contemplate about the church I see a lot of work that needs to be done but at the same time I sense a bright future ahead. Which affects me physically tying knots in my stomach even as I write this, I wonder is it your way of saying yes it has a bright future, yes we are doing your work obediently, yes as long we lift your name great things will happen, yes there will be trials but be faithful you will come out stronger. We will be the fish that swims against the current of the world and at end of that stream I know will find you so in the name of Jesus I pray Amen!

Prayer for God's Will in my life

I seek your wisdom and ministry in life, I open myself to you, nothing escapes your sight so I know that you've seen what's in my heart but unlike before I open my heart to you as I do and your spirit comes to me it honours me and feels me with peace with your love comforting me. For when you reside in me I welcome it and say you are home, teach me what holds me from further advancing take over and break my visage mend it stronger and shape it how it should be.

Prayer for Wisdom

I pray God for understanding and wisdom as I read your word many things escape me but I know you'll see me through it for you are faithful to those who believe in you and serve you. Prayer is our weapon you have given us I am thankful for what I have understood of your word it has been a guiding light to me and answered questions and enlightened to things I did not know and as a new convert challenge my way of thinking so I can be closer to you and live life the way I'm supposed to. It has shown me how to be humble, how to pray to you, and the cost of sin and how it affects my way of living. So I pray father that you use me for what you have made me for. I pray that you show me my destiny so I can embrace it obediently & cheerfully, I pray speak to me Lord show me your face place a burden you want me to carry for your glory Amen!

Talking 2 God: Rebuking

Outwardly and inwardly I have begun to change which that devil has noticed and has attacked me from every angle possible and more so in my isolation ha but I belong to you so let the light of your truth be shun on him and let that light reveal his lies and let that truth snare him and send him back to the pit and those lies bring a curse to him that stays his tongue from further speaking against you to me amen.

Talking 2 God: Looking inward

Know when I look at myself I wonder what is lacking in me or holds me back from doing God's will more effectively so I pray that you show me anything that I need to work on for I want to continue to grow and be closer to you and more like Christ because if I do not do this then and I become content with the way I am then, there would not movement forward no strengthening of my faith, with me feeling a great distance between us and in thinking I'm fine the way I am pride will set in which could lead me to fall away no longer bearing fruit but amongst the thorns, but in prayer I cry out show me father what is in me that stops growth and cast it away.

Talking 2 God: Blazing Soul

O blessed one in reverence of your greatness am I. Instruct me on true righteousness and reveal to me the flaming sword that at a single gaze strikes fear in the hearts of the wicked that cuts thru iniquity scorching it into ash. To those who follow and you have kept let it be a blazing flame of hope, reveal thy purpose that my soul be quenched of its thirst feed my hungry mind with wisdom, filter out folly and wrongdoing humble and bring humility to my heart and reveal and cleanse me of pride and arrogance. To what can I attribute to myself? Can a man achieve purity and holiness without God and if he claims to then who does he compare himself to with such assertions? Anoint and bless me Lord work your purpose thru me and walk with me in spirit all the days of my mortal life Amen.

Talking 2 God: From Cloud 9 to Reality

As a daydreamer most of my thoughts are trivial and just nonsense but the one thing that I do think about is that I am accountable for the things I do here on earth and that one day you will open the book of life and read me my life and Judge me I know words will escape but I will accept responsibility for what I've done as a faithful son I ask for forgiveness Amen.

Talking 2 God: Hopeful

My desire is to know you to see your face for I am your son. I rebelled but now I am obedient your will. When I sleep I hope you have angels watching over me and that your divine spirit gives me the sweetest dreams, sun rises and sets and the days a short for me so for you they must move in the blink of an eye so I await patiently for your word to reach me and my destiny to be revealed. I'll never be able to fathom your love but I know when I bleed, cry out in pain or find myself in sorrow that you weep for me and you care and that you will comfort me. Such a thought makes the bad cloudy days feel better as your love clears the clouds in sky and reveals a beautiful sun so how can I remain in bad state? The answer I cannot you're there for me, you provide for me you counsel me so I won't let my faith break I won't let my stumbles in life keep down Amen.

Talking 2 God in prayer

Lord I humble myself before your presence as I engage you in a rhetorical conversation about my thoughts, your word as gave thought-provoking revelations, in the past I was never saved so most never reached me I dismissed it or faded in out while it was preached. I see now with eyes now open as for the first time my sin and the power of your salvation, how wise your word his with the personal growth I'm undergoing in my walk of faith.

Talking 2 God: Foot Solider

God I willingly receive your son and in doing so he has saved me and renewed me best way I can describe it is that it's a comfort and that I've joined the winning team like I was supposed to, now I'm just a foot solider awaiting his command and in the mean while I pray read your word and work at your house of worship and strengthen my relationship with you and be ready for the day you call on me amen.

Pray to the Almighty One

In the deepest rumination of mind & soul you have reached the unreachable changed the unchangeable, shaped and placed them in the correct path amongst the worst you have proved your sovereignty over all your will is perfect. You have my trust & faith you have my life in your hands though my eyes won't always remain dry you'll be there to wipe my tears away Amen.

Talking 2 God: Eyes open

You know every so often when I walk around now as a follower of Christ and sin has been more noticeable and when I speak to people without judgment of course and see what sins hold them back from you presence, makes me think how can I reach this person will they not turn on me if I speak your name its often seen as offensive to suggest to someone that they need to be put right with God for that says to them that they are sinners which means when they die a real hell is waiting for them and they see themselves as good so scornfully reject your love & your ways.

Others see my faith and your teachings as fantasy and irrelevant, in those times I ask for your guidance and that you speak to them thru me for if it were left to me without the Holy Spirit would I not be on their side for I have been saved by your Grace, and given the Holy Spirit to help so in those situations I pray for help to find the right words even if it is to plant seed in them through a few words that one day make great impact, Shakespeare once said **"what's in a name that which we call a rose by any other name would smell just as sweet"** and as a God who cares for every individual because we are created by a loving God you will reach all individuals Amen.

Talking 2 God: My Heartbeat

My heart concerning things of God had no beat the empathy towards victims of evil & suffering was drowned out by continuous exposure to its never ending cycle, and its inability to be dealt with. Revive my heart and teach it to feel the way it should and to conquer the evil within first Amen.

Prayer of Fear & Hope

Lord hear my prayer I fear the lust of my flesh, covetousness and at times my lack of empathy and embrace of apathy because without your spirit I would stray and be separated from you so I pray that your will done in my life and cast away the things that bind me & keep me from drawing closer to you Lord. When my flesh lusts for a woman to know her am I not committing adultery with such a thought? Sin which then pulls me away from your sight, but there is hope because thanks to your ministry and guidance through the Holy Spirit when the feeling of lust begins to overwhelm me I do not feed those thoughts I simply turn away and let them starve. When I covet my flesh begins to justify why it's right as way of denial and to continue in such sin but again your spirit speaks to me and reminds how sin offends you so I say to myself "is that what I want to, offend God?" who has given me life by GIVING his son to die for my sins. I Pray against my flesh and continue to praise & worship happily and remain faithful to his word and so I can one day be there in the place you have prepared for me... after I die And my body will decay and left to the worms and the rest to the earth that even the flowers placed at my grave will die. So I do not wish to waste time sinning, I will continue to be a servant for you and alas I will have eternal life after death so in the name of Jesus I pray Amen!

Talking 2 God: Plea of Guidance

I pray for it keeps my heart clean; your word gives wisdom you have given me the instruments in which to keep me upright. You have provided the only angle in which a man can stand straight I will not pray haughty prayers nor distort the wisdom you have blessed me with, prayer tends to the soul your wisdom is infinite yet my days are numbered therefor never will there be a time I do not require thy wisdom see to me Lord turn your gaze on my concerns Amen.

Chapter 2: Poetic Proverbs of My Faith

Conviction

God I pray to thee lend your ear I have been given life through your son pray to you thankful having been reborn and cleansed of my iniquity. The sacrifice of my Lord and saviour was a great debt I can never truly repay or say enough thanks to such is the greatness of our Salvation. With your spirit dwelling in me, edifies me in my walk of faith as I attempt to be more like my saviour and draw closer to you.

No longer do I relish in the things of the world nor look for sustenance in it for such things are evil and temporary when feeding the flesh but lead to an eternal perdition, a place where I am without you. So with your spirit in tow I gain willpower to resist the temptation and thus hope to gain your favour & everlasting love.

My God

As I rest the angels of the Lord watch over me, in my dreams he speaks to me with counsel, I awake from such dreams with peace of mind for my God loves me and speaks to me. I have faith for it is said; **John 14:2 My Father's house has many rooms; if that were not so, would I have told you that I am going there to prepare a place for you?** Therefore when I give I will give gladly without whining and serve obediently with love.

Rejoice

Rejoice for the truth has set you free while the lies of the devourer had you ensnared, so I say it is important that when you look in the mirror look beyond your flesh and into your heart and be truthful to yourself and to God. Receive the son provided for our salvation that his love reaches you his spirit comfort you, by then simply preaching of the hope within you will become one his ministers.

The Soul

What is a soul & what shape does it hold? One exists within me attached to this earthly vessel of flesh and bone; I have yet to set my eyes on it. Yet to feel it like I feel the beating of my heart the irony is how populace claims to have been born with nothing & pursue the things of the world and yet never take a moment in reflection to think that they have always had what was most valuable. How do I know there's such a thing? In my Salvation & rebirth I believe it is there thru faith of my saviour and not sight as it is said "**2 Corinthians 5:7: For we walk by faith not by sight**", plus personal experience with prayer as further affirmed this to those who do not believe they label me an anti-intellectual for placing faith above conventional wisdom of man I hold my tongue and do not curse them. For to do so would be iniquities does it not say in: "**Jude 1: 22 be merciful to those who doubt**" Instead I rebuke their words in prayer however keep prayer for their living souls.

Responsibility

It is unwise to dwell on mistakes as it is to try and make too many excuses for them, to do so only ends with turning away and running such things should not be for a servant of God.

Deceitful Seduction

It has an alluring aroma and calls to me with a soothing lullaby as I reach it & embrace it, never does it fulfil me thus I seek its embrace ever more than before and an endless pursuit begins. But I was a fool for it was a snare on my soul by the adversary, the alluring aroma has turned into the stench of death unable am I to take a breath without it assaulting my senses. Soothing lullaby turns into a song of damnation that demons rejoice in as I cry out in vain while its embrace binds me like shackles. For I did not gain what I sought rather reaped what I had sown for all the days of my life I fed desires of the flesh now I see how iniquities and empty that quest was weighing it against my eternal soul.

Unseen answer

The answers may be simple but the journey to see the answers in our own lives is where there's struggle, pain and suffering, that chips away at the soul. I put my soul in the hands of God he will shield my soul even if my flesh is struck, he is everlasting, he is invisible yet is glory and spirit leaves a visible print in this world, open your eyes to the possibility of his existence that he can lead you to the unseen answer in your life.

Love is God's Gift

As I look out see mankind I tend to focus on its sin and blemishes more so than its capacity for love Thy not see the way a mother can love her children; or a husband his wife at this instant put God in the blend does then not our capacity for love then become boundless by his love of us what then would hold us back? The enemy of our souls? No! His lies will be exposed for the entire world to see and the truth set us free. Would we not then gain eternal life thru Christ rather than perish as we rightful should, therefore may the love of Christ reach all.

Mind & Heart

Rescue me from the oppression of skepticism of the mind, save me from the intellectual resistance of the mind, bring down the barriers of wickedness of the heart and open me to the wonder of Your glory re-introduce me to the fear of God and show me the definition of what it truly means to love, bridge the gap between the head and the heart so as not to be led by a mere feeling or knowledge alone, carve this into my essence and make it everlasting.

Fellowship

Fellowship is it not an important aspect of our faith? Coming together at the house of the Lord to worship and mingle in the things of God in honesty. For we should be truthful, do not deceive me with a façade which covers your discouragement for such behaviour is a folly listen if you are dejected share it with me when I am joyful I will share it with you should fault fall on you for a transgression I will forgive you and be it trouble should find you can rely on me for more than Just a prayer.

What We Have

The basis of our trust in Christ it keeps your soul at peace, guides your path even though you may not always know where, yet you do not doubt the shepherd that leads you for one thing is revealed what lies at the end of the path. Speak aloud that others may hear what is it that you have.

Gifts of God

Each one of us has a God given gift that comes in many forms whether it's musical talent, Strength, kindness or Gifts of the spirit these I call "the things that are" The things that aren't, can be suppressed, the rest I do not know of but I leave it to God; such is the world as I have come to see it.

Impossible

Which of these statements are truly impossible? For a man to lick his elbow or his chin, sneeze with your eyes open, tickle yourself. Gain true understanding of the cosmos, be a good man or on the Day of Judgment present a case why you didn't believe in God and why you should still enter his kingdom?

Verdant and Blooming

Timid as she appears a great strength in her she has thanks to you Jesus you bring out the best in her, so as you continue to work inwardly you plan to raise her up thus affecting her outwardly. Her voice will be one of strength, clarity and wisdom that will carry thru to all rows of Grand halls & theatres. Her posture will be dignified showing the authority you have given her, your spirit within her will give her a strong presence among others. Her growth in faith will never be impeded she whole-heartedly has faith in you; she prays for your ministry is obedient & has the support of her congregation. All her worries you will put to rest, I myself will keep her in my prayers and keep my eyes on her lest I miss seeing her Bloom for truly the greatest miracles you have performed are in transforming hearts of mankind. To a positive force for good in the worship of your Glory for her true beauty will be seen in a life dedicated to you **For Life itself is an expression of worship**[1] when living in faith and there you will find true beauty and love.

Man should not be alone

Is it not true that as men that thru you we find love, peace & salvation however the flesh aches for love of a wife, even though they can be the bane that takes **the mind at end of its tether**[2]. Even so such love whole-heartily given completes our brief existence in this earthly visage, good though that such love is brief for it brings more appreciation to it. And some relief for alas how much more can an exhausted mind of a man take of a woman, Good it is if you are right with the Lord as he will grant eternal peace.

1. Dr Ravi Zacharias RZIM
2. H. G. Wells

Stench

O how sinners speak with such pride, though the airs of their words are like putrid flatulence causing me to drastically flinch back with my hand to my nose, for their boastful talk of a life of sin does not attract me for I do not despise them instead weep for them for I wish to save their living souls and keep them in prayer Till the day they are saved by Jesus for I have faith such a time will come meanwhile I offer them counsel & a Tic Tac lest I spew my lunch.

Wonderful counsellor

Finally the foundations of my house are solid; that which you built for me all is left is to maintain it you have provided the tools & the blueprints, thank you Jesus my wonderful instructor nobody as lived a life as beautiful as you and I aim to emulate such greatness **ho kurios mou kai ho Theos mou**[3].

Serving

I take my needs out of the equation what do you desire of me, how may I serve your kingdom for I know not what the future holds so I will have faith that the decisions I make will be guided towards your will, so when I sit back I can say this is where I'm meant to be.

Myself

I look thru myself only to find iniquity only thru you can I be saved the I which was and the I that I am now clash having lost some battles; but with your spirit residing in me I can win the war the spirit will conquer the flesh.

---

3. Greek literarily means "My Lord and My God"

Beloved

I wonder how you are, many seasons have passed since I last laid eyes on you, since I heard your voice, you whose name is "beloved"

I wonder how much changed about you for alas me well I'm a whole new individual thanks to Christ now a new concern arises that of your eternal soul which I pray for to be saved as mine has been.

I wonder if you know that from now on I will keep you in my prayers for healing of your affliction & salvation I wonder if you know the days that we reside in this mortal coil are short beyond death there is eternity waiting with two places waiting to be occupied you may jest that such things are a fantasy but take heed and soften your heart and let God minister to you for the price for such thoughts is high.

I wonder If you know my heart can be broken by that thought that you are going to the place below then imagine how God your creator who defined love gave it to us as a gift feels do know you what that means **with love comes the freedom to not love**[4]. That is what you have been given so will you continue to reject or pursue truth for I believe you will find Jesus is the answer to all your problems if you wholeheartily seek him.

Hmmm I wonder if you know…….

Prayer Life

A life of Prayer to pray before I eat to prayer before I sleep, to pray for forgiveness to prayer for my family & friends, prayers of gratitude, to pray in times of distress, to pray in times of joy. This and all things in my life I wish to make routine with Prayer, A life of prayer is what I seek to which will bring me closer to God.

---

4. Dr Ravi Zacharias RZIM

My Focus

"**My focus determines my reality**[5]?" then I will focus on you Lord for you are the truth; "**Genesis 1:1: In the Beginning God.**" for before there was anything there was you and your existence is outside of time and perfect; "**Revelation 22:13: I am The Alpha and The Omega. The beginning and The End, The First and The Last.**" None can be greater than you, I serve an eternal almighty God who loves me and is faithful to me who asks only that I love him and be faithful too for his definition of love transcendence our understanding; "**John 3:16: For God so loved the world that he gave his only begotten son, that whoever believes in him should not perish but have everlasting life.**"

Inner Beauty

She is beautiful like a rose and like the rose one must be careful of the thorns, for her beauty clouds her judgment for she relies on that giving her a false sense of entitlement thus I say look inwardly, is what you see inwardly as beautiful? Has no one ever told you a rose eventually withers losing its beauty leaving nothing behind but a memory that is forgotten when another rose blooms. Be attentive, I speak with the love of the Lord in my heart and do not judge only offer counsel humble yourself For the Lord's gaze is focused on your heart.

New Convert

As I mediate and study on the word the voice of an old Chinese man in English speaks to me "oh young one stirr ("still") wet behind ears Thu art in the way of Christ" and it is so, the standard is high and to fall from it is a mighty fall indeed. So let it be that his spirit sustains me and his word guide. "**Psalms 1:2-3; But whose delight is in the law of the Lord, and meditates on his law day and night. He shall be like a tree planted by the rivers of water that brings forth its fruit in its season, whose leaf also shall not wither; and whatever he does shall prosper.**"

5. Star Wars Episode 1: Phantom Menace.

Falsehood will not prevail

There's a poem I heard quite a few times that's worth a mention;

"Oh pitiful shadow lost in the darkness, Bringing torment and pain to others. Oh damned soul, wallowing in your sin...Perhaps... it is time to die."6

To which I say no, for thru Christ we are given eternal life: Thru self-adulation I was destined for eternal despair Alas you plucked from perdition gave me eternal life showed me the way man ought to live and It so that thru the wisdom of scripture I no longer bring Torment to others or wallow in my sin but dedicated my life to God's Agenda.

True Strength

I read the word & pray hoping to build strong faith for how strong was David's faith when facing Goliath, when staying his hand from slaying Saul an anointed man of God. How strong was Daniel's faith when thrown in the lion's den? I cannot be certain or neither do I know of anyone with such faith who in that situation wouldn't defecate a brick. And what of the founder's faith when being tempted by the evil one in the desert, for how many have fallen for his lie.

Seeking God

I seek you first Lord in doing so your world stands stretched out before my eyes. The Holy Spirit in tow in my walk and in my dreams I will fear not and want not and need not. Thru your spirit I Conquer and bear conviction of your glory and the Truth of your word. **"Philippians 4:13; I can do all this through him who gives me strength"**

---

6. Hell Girl by Miyuki Etō

God's will not mine

Just because I proclaim my actions & decisions that I have made to be for God, does not mean it is his will. For the vision the lord has for me is more wonderful then any I can think of so I must not lose heart for it will be revealed to me in good time in keeping in faith, prayer and reading of his word it shall be so. For all the challenges this world has me, myself and I is the greatest overcoming my sin what greater challenge is there to fall short would mean death. Alas I am not alone my saviour lives within me and died for my sins and baptized me putting the old me to rest, raising me renewed thus his spirit ministers to me keeping me from falling short of his glory so I will continue to fight the good fight, **"Philippians 3:14; I press on toward the goal to win the prize for which God has called heavenward in Christ Jesus."**

Pursuit of a humble heart

 I pray give me insight, knowledge and take away my pride that is so self-serving. It robs me blind of your grace how I'm I to serve humbly when all think of is myself, so I pray edify me Lord reveal my iniquity that I may cast it away and in doing so would help me to understand your will that I may fulfil it as I live my life. **"Proverbs 3:6; in all your ways submit to him, and he will make your paths straight."**

Heaven

Heaven what words can I borrow describe such paradise its glory & beauty cannot be grasped by mankind. Even so we still in are human limitation we imagine this utopia and the wonders it holds but to no avail for no mind or peripheral point of view can ever apprehend power and glory that the kingdom of God holds.

The story of life

The stage was set before the beginning of time you ask how was there a stage before the beginning of time? He was before there was a beginning and knew how the story would unfold from our choices in the freedom given. Therefore as the author of life you wrote an incredible narrative in which the Supreme ethic is Love & Worship of the Lord brings all things together when man fell and destined to die he gave us a saviour and by him we now have a guiding example of how man ought have lived and thru him we are brought to the father given life, redemption and restored from our fall.

The strength to smile

One thing is clear to me we are saved by your grace thanks to Jesus's sacrifice our debt of sin is paid in full and we are reborn but we must remain cautious. For the flesh still may be led astray in our walk as followers of Christ as we encounter trials, alone we cannot win the good fight for the weakness of sin is still in us but Christ dwells in us too and is stronger, no matter how much we stumble he will keep picking us up. And through fellowship with our fellow believers who are on the same journey, we form strong bonds in your name.

We support each other to best of our ability with the help of the scriptures & the Holy Spirit giving us guidance as we do the work of God. No man has any knowledge what tomorrow will bring alas if you have faith in God do not worry about what tomorrow may bring and put yourself out there for God and even though you're weak thru Christ you'll naturally attain strength & conviction. That's how you'll be able to smile and live strong despite the trials and tribulations that is what I think having the Joy of the Lord in my life is.

Flower of Faith

Let this flower of faith blossom once and for all in all of mankind and in the name of Christ let it flourish for eternity for those who believe ne'er shall they tire of such sight of its beauteous visage.

Men

Insecurity lies in men without God it is they that find pride in might and lavish in lustful pursuit of woman & money and material possessions, they grow with a wrong sense of what it takes to be a man and what in this world holds true value. Duplicitous in nature no shame no sense of accountability with pain and more insecurity their hearts harden and their speech is that of bitter drunkards. Lord let not my heart stray from your ways for I know how easy it is to turn into that type of man, keep me, bless me, anoint and instruct me.

Burden of a traitorous mind

Why is it that my words & actions define me but my thoughts betray me at every possible turn am I truly destined for damnation or is this trial that I must overcome? If it is so Lord I pray strengthen my heart & mind for the ways of the world calls sin natural accepting it, but I seek to purge such evil or must I endure such vile torment as for greater purpose? I await for your word. **Psalms 34:17; the righteous cry out, and the Lord hears them; he delivers them from all their troubles**.

Burning Faith & Dying Faith

We gather together souls each with burning flame of faith our flame unified & burning strong for the things of God, the enemy of our souls schemes and leads, astray a single soul gusting icy wind of prevarication smothering its flame.

Breath of Life

I thank you God for every breath that I've taken in, one being better than the last, for you have given me life in every breath. For before I found you each breath I took in was of death each worse than the last, taking life rather than giving.

Words

You and I by our own words dig a shallow grave and bury ourselves in it when speaking in jealousy and in speaking with delight in our hearts against those who sin in the ways we do not, for to do so will impede our growth in faith. Pride of life will set in to our hearts and sin will follow slithering in like that duplicitous snake in the garden with those infamous words; "did God really say that? 7"

My Heart for God

I accept all that you say; I accept all that you judge to be upright and that which you claim to be wrongdoing, I proclaim in prayer look in to my heart Lord judge me for I have claimed from my lips to ears of those who listen to be upright by surrendering to your love & repenting of my sins kneeling down at the Cross of Jesus Christ and living by faith. So I pray have you found any wrongdoing in my heart if so let it be revealed that I may repent and may it be that you cleanse my heart of such wrongdoing, for as you see in my heart I live for you and such vile does not belong in me as I walk the path of faithful servant.

All Mighty

It is said that fear does not come from God; only God fearing is Godly, **Proverbs 1:7; the fear of the Lord is the beginning of knowledge, but fools despise wisdom and instruction.** So allow the Lord to strengthen your heart and accept your weakness for the Lord will allow you to work wonders in his name and your imperfections will be a testimony to others who are discouraged about their imperfections, believe in the God who believes in you without fearing the judgment of others only His is the judgment that matters in the end. **"Proverbs 3:5; trust in the Lord with all your heart and lean not on your own understanding."**

---

7. Genesis 3:1

Thank you is never enough

I will follow you wherever, if could I would go where you are now if it were possible I would offer you counsel if it were possible I would take on my responsibility of my sins rather than sacrificing you Alas it cannot be so, dedicating myself to your cause and seeking you with all my heart using my life to leave your mark on this world that others may see me and glorify thy Holy name.

Weakness within

I pray for I overestimated myself, in believing in you I subconsciously set myself above sin and in doing so left my guard down for sin is a weakness in mankind's spirit. Then I began to slip from the smaller standards and I doubted myself. Therein lies the problem, for subconsciously I still overestimated my own capacity, Like a blind man wanting to pour himself a glass of water without having someone to stop him from overfilling that glass.

And so I continued to slip till I reached a point where the thought came in "maybe it's not me it's God" wow look at that what a mighty slip that was! With realising what has happened I humble myself & repent and having learned a little something about myself there and why it's said were saved by grace not by our own volition.

Protection

Deliver me from the devourer, keep me from the hands of the wicked and let the thieves that come in the night as I sleep pass me by for I am under your protection. Let your spirit soften my heart so I may be more forgiving to those who have wronged me, shake me out of apathy and lead me to a life of conviction.

Upright

A righteous servant of God does not look down on lost souls him/her only doing so as to help them up and show the truth of Christ, for that lost soul to arise and also be righteous in the eyes of the Lord.

Living & Walking Faith

Do their eyes not reflect the conviction they proclaim for it's said "the eyes are the window to the soul" in those eyes should be a reflection of our faith that others may see. We are called to mirror Christ so does your manner match his? When you walk amongst the people are you recognised as his follower? Do you influence lost souls or are you influenced by them, meditate where does thy heart lie?

The Journey

The journey of heaven has begun and began when I accepted Christ in my life for the life I lived before was all to gain a footing to that starting point. Now filled with hope and love of God I submit to him pray and wait for my destiny to be revealed for "any willing servant desires to fulfil the will of his master" and my master, my father, my redeemer, my comforter & friend deservers all the Glory and praise for his way is a holy way so I follow his way.

Dreamer

You dreamed this universe into existence, you dreamed of the earth and its horizon and set it into place, you saw your own image and dreamed of it in mortal form for a purpose and for your Glory I ask of thee grant me the privilege of becoming the man you dreamed of before the beginning, outside of time, when you first dreamed of a dream.

Pride

Pride corrupts your soul, a corrupt soul distorts your heart & a distorted heart leads to sin and sin leads to death, soften your heart and let Jesus minister to you.

The Call

When I heard the call of you in my heart I fought and ignored stepping away from your sight to not be found for to cast-off your love hurts me more than you for I have lost something by rejecting you but who can keep from you what you seek or desire and so you continue to call on me. And in my heart of hearts I said to you; "so why should I give up this life why is it iniquities? Am I not free to live as I wish? Must I live with such rules?" and that is how it begun. Further you kept on calling through my friend and through your word explaining to me how sin works and the morality that is in your word is sound and without fault. No longer was it a question of understanding but of my lack of faith and in my heart of hearts I say to you "cannot escape from you I feel a call from you but is it you or just I, chasing shadows and descending in to darkness of religion?" The veil lifted I saw the world as it truly was looking at it under the law of God and doing so I saw in me was an unwilling heart holding me back for the sins I pursued enjoyed is what kept me from believing and taking that step of faith and now I say to you; " you have reached my heart of hearts thus I kneel down and proclaim I'm a sinner and I need a saviour I accept Christ as my Lord and saviour come in to my heart show me your real and I will serve you till death and beyond even that".

First class ticket to paradise

My final destination is heaven that's what is promised to me; he saved me and has a place for me at his house of many mansions. The day will arrive when I take that journey to the other side no check in luggage, no carry on either for this's a one way trip and all I need is with him. But I do pray that there's no queue or monotonous security measures just a relaxing first class ride to that Final Destination to my true home free from my wickedness and sin.

Contamination

I was once told that; "Fear contaminates your faith" and I have found it to be so and it is repeatedly said in the scriptures "Fear not", for that fear will always hold you back from following God's will and so I pray that the Lord may bless with valour for what's in store in the unknown future.

Praise the Lord

This Mortal frame is defined by you in effect; my being calls for me to glorify you for when I see clear blue sky it calms my spirit. How a setting sun puts me in a trance of its fiery orange glow as it slowly descends to not be seen again till morn. How you made the palette of taste that not only satisfies my hunger but brings joy starting at tongue ending at soul, joy & sustenance in full circle in the act of eating. How you gave us the gift of love and that all relationships are built on love and are sacred.

And thru marriage of man and woman we are able consummate that love through a beautiful physical act complementing their individuality while also joining as one and in doing so bringing new life into the world. How music you created allowed us to express the deepest feelings of our souls allowing us also to enjoy all things through its mellifluous melodies to all this I say glory to God may the angels in heaven praise our Holy Father.

The Struggles

Life gets hard to smile through when it asks of you to bend over and grab your ankles, in those times I go through the experience of violent impulses thank God that his spirit is with me and offers me counsel and clarity and comfort in such times for I can imagine where I would be without him in such times. **Psalm 62:1-2: Truly my soul silently waits for God; From Him comes my salvation. He only is my rock and my salvation; He is my defense.**

Questions

My mind races with questions of suffering, injustice and evil, my thoughts guide me within I see my comfort and safety. Yet when I hear or see real suffering, injustice and evil in the lives of others they find the strength to have faith and I see my comfort, safe keeping as truly fooled me for the Lord as blessed me and kept me. Trouble eludes me, comfort & safety know me well as friends I have enjoyed foods & pleasures that this world offers yet I question God about the state of the world truly I have been foolish. I repent and ask forgiveness for the Lord loves all and is Holy there is no fault in him, I must amend my mind and exercise true faith like Jesus leave all in his hands for no human can truly solve the problems this world has and I say praise the Lord for he has blessed me and kept me.

Let God correct your path

A man rejecting God runs against gale force winds, a follower of Christ condemning others goes against the very teachings that offer him salvation, so to those who reject God reproach yourselves, let the wind carry you and let Jesus be your wings. To those who claim to be a follower and betray the teachings humble yourself and repent so that you may be forgiven, come forth to God's well of life drink of it and let it rejuvenate your faith.

Shadow Humour

Now that my eyes are open to the truth I remain diligent of the lies, humorous they are as if told by a clown, the father of lies is like a dog watch God as he chases his tail. He hides in the darkness but you shine a light in the darkness that casts a wide shadow, using my hands I make shapes: Parrot, frog and duck. Because if I am with you I need not fear only remain cautious.

The Truth

You may make fun of it, you may cheapen it, this redemption provided but only love, only desires and only you're true self have any real meaning thru him I won't let that reality go! Everything and anything this world has is only worth having with the Lord's blessing so you may make fun of it, you may cheapen it but you'll never destroy it. The Lord will grant me a spear of light to pierce thru the void of darkness he'll grant me wisdom to reach your heart for there's a cure for sin his name is Jesus so for your own sake don't make fun of it, don't cheapen it the redemption provided.

My Perspective

The heart of me, the strength of me, the life of me, the good of me and the love of me, all the things are in me that are pure & righteous are only so because you are the Lord of me and the God of me. Sow your spirit to my soul let your radiance purify the wickedness that lies within.

Miracle

He can look into my heart & soul and see who I really am beneath the face people see and chose to keep me, love me, forgive me and has a purpose for me and place for me beyond the mortal frame. He instructs me although some lessons are painful, the hand he places on me may be heavy but he has not given me anything he knows I can't handle. He knows what I desire but will provide what I need, beyond sadness, beyond the joy and beyond my heartbeat lays eternal love, glory, worship, praise and communion with God a freely gifted miracle given to mankind and we only have to accept the Son delivered to us.

Left handed view & hidden Right hand

I am called to faith I will believe that if your spirit is not to the right of me it's to the left of me and I keep hold of my heart to not deviate left or right of your ways, are you not my umpire? Are you not my conductor?

Villain & Hero

I'll be a villain to pain in times I come upon hardship in spiritual & physical form by praising the Lord knowing in life or death he'll be with me. I'll hold high the flag of truth every time my faith is placed upon a firing squad of those who hate the truth and underneath the villain in me & the blazing inferno of faith in my soul that runs down to my bone marrow. The spirit of my saviour will work thru me to reach lives as a blessing in disguise for both me and the individual he calls by name that lost Sheep he leaves the 99 to retrieve.

Subtleties of Life

You have saved me even with the little subtleties of life that I love and just the same take for granted till I take time to reflect on my life and see them, relatable songs that uplift my spirit until I'm unable to contain myself. Those awe inspiring movies of underdog heroes prevailing over evil & injustice showing how vast and articulate the depths of the ocean of human imagination go. The simple but delightful food, how it sparks a sense of nostalgia of a romanticized memory when such a particular food became a notable favourite to serve as a pick me up. Those secret indulgences that our own because of our unique character, the things we find funny that others don't, conversations among friends that bring joy and the true meaning of fellowship. Couples with their tender sweet nothings soft spoken in secret such things seem small in measure but in scale weigh a ton.

I'm calling on the behalf of Jesus

I dial the number to reason to testify of the truth but on the other line contempt answers and begins a notorious barrage of profanity towards me and the truth although offended, my heart is weighed down by such a closed off heart I end the call with peace be with you. In prayer the Lord Counsels me telling me not to Judge my endeavour a failure for I have shared the word and planted the seed and the rest is within God's perfect will I must trust in him in all things.

The Vulture

I must be dying for I see a vulture circling me in the sky its wing span cast a dark shadow over me even if I do not look up the shadow lets me know it's there, is my time nigh? Was my pursuit in life just dying to live or living to die? Lord I pray if you are the living God let your voice reach me before I perish for I do not fear that the vulture will devour my flesh upon my death I fear what lays in wait beyond death **Job 14:14 if man dies shall he live again?**

The eye

Your lying eyes betray you and blind you from the truth look to God to show you the point of view that your eyes should see, looking thru the eyes with a conscience instead of looking thru the eyes devoid of conscience following a mere feeling that betrays you, a lie will not sustain you. Think of the hourglass of your life if you pursue a feeling you'll never be satisfied you will resent that your days are numbered but if you recognise Gods ways and pursue them you'll be joyous for your days are numbered till you stand in his kingdom.

How many Beans make 5?

Am I the witless wonder? Am I the moronic man who bit into candy-bar that turned out to be a bar of soap? Am I the half-wit that tries to draw a one ended stick? Or am I the obtuse one who tries to draw a square-circle? Goes without saying one must have knowledge the world does not take kindly to the simpleminded but can knowledge of this world in itself take you to moral absolutes that must not be violated? **Deuteronomy 8:3 man shall not live by bread alone but man lives by every word that proceeds from the mouth of the Lord.**

Patience

I made prayers of many concerns and it has been advised to me patience is the key if so bless me with the key Lord and show me the door that I may unlock making my escape of this room and be endowed with patience as I dwell in the room of forbearance.

Blade

I will not harden my heart against you Lord for you took my soul which was like a rusted & dull blade you removed the rust and cleaned it till your reflection could be seen. You sharpened me to a fine point that should iniquity reach out and simply touch my soul it shall be cut. All this you have done for me because you love me so I will not harden my heart against you Lord.

Diagnoses: Sin!

We wrestle with God within this physical frame and assassinate the mind first then our very soul how is this done? When we renounce God's ways and seek an incoherent frame of thought to which we build a life thinking of it as coherent while it actually fools us to incite the wickedness of our heart. As those who believe such things celebrate with us as if in renouncing God we have been freed but really were led astray slowly but surely for we have been enslaved you cannot build solid ground to stand on with a lie. So as the years go by the lie crumbles beneath our feet, the sound and sight of rubble falling away brings the realization of leading an incoherent life to the point of debauchery, as we believed to be sovereign over our own lives leaves our feet planted in mid-air. But the God we so joyfully renounced provided the diagnoses, man is too possessed by himself seeks ways to deify himself and in other to fill that God size emptiness pursues all things with the wrong point of reference all on the basis that it feels right! But instead poisons his soul leading to an ultimate ruthless slaying of it to which God weeps at the very loss for to every individual he has placed intrinsic worth. Looking at the mirror that reflects the soul ask yourself will I not prostrate and surrender to the author of life who out of love provided redemption for all in the image of Christ and have my soul saved then healed?

Thread

Intertwined by a thread of desire for I sleep to dream & dream of dreams from dreams to reality for as I wake towards what I dream I walk to.

The Night

O wicked man the darkness of the night comforts thee, in the night while there is none in sight you plot vile things, in the night you carry out evil doing-ins, in the night you seek refuge from those thou hast trespassed. O wicked man know that the night shall rob thee of sight Know the night shall rob thee of sanity know the night shall devour thy flesh and claim thy soul.

Valour

Steel this heart of mine Lord for the coming days that hope is not in sight when the shadow of evil can be seen in approach thus as long thou never forsake me I will not perish but have everlasting life ho kurios mou kai ho theos mou.

Tomorrow

The sun does not rise for iniquity nor does a day go by for its sake tomorrow never comes for the lost prostrate yourself. Surrender thy will to thy creator do so as a desperate desire in thy heart & awake for today is now tomorrow and from this new day God will tend to thy soul so breathe in the air of salvation and enjoy all the days to come for they bring victory.

Finitude

I won't deny Lord the tides of the heart sway in many directions and its finitude cannot be contained by man alone. **Genesis 4:7: Sin lies at the door and its desire is for you, but you should rule over it.** Give strength and wisdom of your spirit to rule over the tides of the heart for many things elude man, without your instruction there will be no peace to hold to. **Job 6:24: Teach me, and I will hold my peace: and if I have been ignorant in anything, instruct me**.

Saviour

Lost in the darkness of life was I Whom could I turn to is there a saviour?

Who can lift my burden from my weary shoulders and hear my plight?

My search is arduous in which truth is relative and nothing is absolute Amidst the perplexing world a voice of reason reaches me.

The Lord answers "Here I am search no further" his timing is that of perfection he awaits till my heart softens.

Waits till I forsake my folly of living as my own God and calls to me "Here I am search no further".

For what man can comprehend the mysteries of the cosmos? What power does man hold that transcends his?

Can God not command the sun to be still? Did he not command the world into existence with words alone?

Do not be flippant when you approach his altar for his love is offered freely and liberates his lost children.

Emptiness

O weary dreary soul of thee hast thou been enthralled by personal cynicism? Hast the eyes of the seductress bewitched thee? Hast thy pursuit of all pleasures numbed thee? What folly, what lie has stricken thee? Leaving only emptiness speak thy mind from thy heart thru thy mouth!

The unwise

Carry yourself accordingly for the idiocy of the world comes in the form of men they judge themselves wise their words are seductive in sound nevertheless deadly in practice. Lord call the names of your sheep that they may recognise your voice that they may gather with every knee bowed down before thee preserve them on the righteous path to fulfil their life purpose.

The Lord of me The God of me

Thou art the master craftsmen in awe of your creation am I. Thou art the original artist and inspiration for all, thou gave us music to express feeling to which mere rhetoric cannot, thou hast written the book of life that which surpasses all a perfect story and narrative for thou hast seen the end in the beginning for greatness & truth lies within yourself. For all of Life is defined by you nothing escapes the grasp of your Holy Hand nothing escapes thy perfect sight and thou art the solution to all problems & conquer all evil.

Thinking about My God

All that I do, is all to worship you though it's all different I know I need your loving spirit every day, my inmost desire is to remain with you loving, worshiping and seeking you ever more. For to do of such helps keep your spirit for all it takes is one moment one indiscretion to lose it all. when I close my eyes I see an image of you and I say to myself I cannot live a life where I am without you my soul prays to you for love & healing open the heavens for thy loving servant.

Salvation

A blessing that cuts thru the curse, love that transforms hearts of hate & despair into hearts of love, makes joy central and pain & suffering peripheral.

Rock

To my friend I vow that I will fight your fights as though they're mine in exchange you will fight for mine. Should you place yourself at risk to protect something so will I, two rock pillars supporting each other's lives & faith. Our words have power, what say you?

Gratitude

The father of lies can no longer deceive me. O how I cried tears of anguish as recognised my sin I repented and was forgiven, his words of forgiveness ring aloud in my ears and I never forget! Salvation given to me, that which I was not worthy, of that mighty sacrifice of Jesus.

Nor is there a vociferous speech or deed to which to payback for that sacrifice made on my behalf God is perpetual in all the promises he has made, Just by bringing perpetual ruin to his enemies, God is infinite and will bring infinite destruction to iniquity, infinite in his love for mankind and slow to anger. Alas I am filled with joy for mighty, holy and sovereign our God is, for with him I am secure and can overcome any predicament this world holds.

Fear

For God says to the fearful; "Rid thyself-of fear", he shall grant thee valor face forward. Stand firm in your fiery conviction, never allow yourself to fall back, retreat and you will weaken, waver and you will perish. Take heed of these words be victorious as you walk in his glory.

Like God?

My friend in your own rumination thou must know that God is real that Jesus took the full brunt of thy burdens, of hate and all sin and died for thee. where dost thy disbelief lie? Seek truth wholly & truly and thou will find it in Christ, for he has spoken it, lived it and died for it. All on the side of truth are with him and are saved souls I assuredly tell the truth that there is a real perdition for those who side with a lie, a place for lost souls a real permanent separation from God. Do not let your soul be lost friend answer the call of God.

Iniquity

Do not be Wily in your speech nor duplicitous in your dealings for such things do not bear fruit. Be mindful for the heavens, know thy heart, what defense will you hold to on the Day of Judgment?

Pain

A life of agony that looks for truth in Christ shall be transformed into a life full of joy & conviction for our Lord & saviour is a star that guides us in the night. The night comes to an end, the day breaks a new Into hope that will never beaten for when day breaks his light of victory is seen. When the night comes his star guides thru the adversity of the Darkness.

Are you not? Will you not? What shall I?

Are you not the God that spoke this universe into existence, formed the earth, divided the light from the darkness & defined all that is on under heaven and earth?

Are you not the Almighty One that made man in your own image, for your own Glory gifted man with love? Defining that love comes with freedom to not love?

Are you not the Blessed One spoken of time after time delivering your faithful servants from plight punishing those who come against your servants and your truth?

Are you not the Holy Father who so loved the world that he GAVE his only begotten son? If so, what will you withhold?

Will you not keep a watchful eye on me or incline your hear to my prayers and keep a light shining on me as I walk into the unknown?

Will you not in your all-knowing mind bring meaning and just resolution in my life?

What shall I then withhold from you? Should I not be grateful and pray for the good health I have, for the food on my plate, for the house I live in and my neighbors also, alas but not least for the son you provided for my salvation?

What shall I do with this heart of mine? Shall I not rebuke the wickedness that lays within waiting to lure me away at every good turn I take? For to embrace it is to rebuke you and choose an eternal separation from you, thus to choose you is to choose to praise and worship and inherit eternal life with eternal communion with you beyond this mortal image.

God Is Watching

Daughter of God your father in heaven is watching over you, your plight does not go unnoticed. Given to you is a loving family whose tears in prayer reach the Heavens. The tears will be wiped away and the heavens will open his spirit will descend & reside in you, for as long as you live never shall you go a day without love for you are safe, you are cherished and wealth in spirit you have been blessed with.

My Fix

Today, yesterday, tomorrow, now and every day is my desire of thy counsel, wisdom and blessing. Just a taste on the tip of my finger is enough to bring zeal of overflowing joy that leaves my body jonesing for more. Today, yesterday, tomorrow, now and every day.

We dared

We dared to dream of sinful longings. We dared to doubt the truth of God. We embraced doubt, birthed a relative truth for ourselves, the new reflection of mankind is that of a hero on to ourselves leading down the road paved with good intentions into damnation for the birth is a still one the reflection a distorted one.

Glory

Apathy stalks me in the form of my own shadow. See to me for it is self-evident a single glance at your silhouette plants a seed of eternal hope in my soul that grows and bears fruit for your glory. How much greater would it be to see you in all your glory in your Fathers celestial Kingdom where not a single shadow can exist.

One of a kind

You are the Gem amongst gems your authenticity and value is immeasurable and no other meets this high standard. If one were to turn their eyes away from you they would never again find that which they found in you in anything else anywhere else.

Holy

If I were to touch your Holy flame would I be consumed by its burning purity? Or would its flames cleanse me of my iniquity? What is it that you see in me? Where do I stand with you? **Psalm 8:4: What is man that You are mindful of him?**

Ambassador of Christ

I pray because I know that you can reach all, for those who are blind let word reach their ears, for those who are deaf let the truth reach them thru sight. As the truth of Jesus Christ reaches them let those who were blind see and those who were deaf hear and be witness to those who are still blind and deaf, and when they explain the hope that is in them let them say "there is one who restores what is lost and grants everlasting life his name is Jesus and He is the saviour of mankind".

En Garde

I won't let the devil have a playground in my mind; I'll be swift & nimble so that his lies strike thin air. I will flex my spiritual muscles with fasting & prayer and the study of your word this I can accomplish with the wisdom, strength and instruction you have blessed me with and continue to bless me with.

Made in the USA
Monee, IL
03 May 2026

49437971R00026